Spark: An Advent Movement

Copyright © 2025 by Charlie Conder

ISBN: 979-8-218-81540-0 (Paperback)

Cover, illustrations, and book design by Abbey Arreguin

Edited by Lauren Sellers and Eric Conder

First printing edition 2025

Charlie Cards
320 M L King Jr Dr SE #13
Atlanta, GA 30312

www.charliecards.com

What is Advent?

It can be easy to assume Advent is just about counting down to Christmas. After all, you may have seen Advent calendars filled with chocolates, cheese, or even skincare products. But it's more than just a countdown or excuse to treat yourself. Advent is a season of reflection as we celebrate the arrival, or advent, of Jesus. We worship a God who isn't far away, but a God who moved into the neighborhood.

Through reflecting on the story of Jesus' arrival and loving as He did, we can experience a meaningful Advent season that helps us connect our faith with action. As we engage in daily spiritual practices and serve those around us, we can experience a lasting transformation that extends far beyond the Advent season.

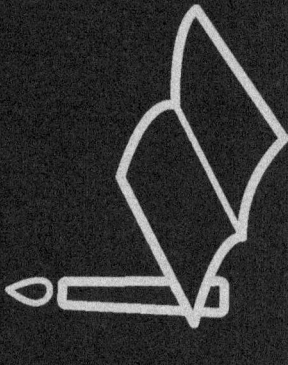

How to Use This Book

This devotion isn't about adding one more thing to your already packed December. It's an invitation to pause for just a few minutes each day and notice where God is at work in and around you. Here's how to make the most of it:

- Find your time. Morning, bus ride, before bed—whenever you can pause and focus.

- Read the provided scripture to experience the story of Christmas.

- Reflect with simple devotion and questions, so you can imagine what Advent means for your everyday life.

- Respond through the daily action because it will give you a way to live out hope, peace, joy, or love through kindness and compassion.

The best way for you to engage in this Advent Experience is whatever way works best for you! You can do the devotional on your own or with a group. You can journal your reflections or reflect in a group chat with a friend. No matter how you engage the experience, the goal is to slow down, reflect, and respond to Advent with open hearts and hands. By Christmas, you'll have practiced the heart of Advent, not just waiting, but actively preparing for the One who makes Christmas matter.

Wait, Who is Coming?

Then Isaiah said, "Listen, house of David! Isn't it enough for you to be tiresome for people that you are also tiresome before my God? Therefore, the Lord will give you a sign. The young woman is pregnant and is about to give birth to a son, and she will name him Immanuel. He will eat butter and honey, and learn to reject evil and choose good. Before the boy learns to reject evil and choose good, the land of the two kings you dread will be abandoned. The Lord will bring upon you, upon your people, and upon your families days unlike any that have come since the day Ephraim broke away from Judah—the king of Assyria." ISAIAH 7:13-17 CEB

READ

Isaiah was a prophet, a minister to King Azariah. He had a ton of influence with the royal court. Isaiah was speaking to the king, who was freaking out. Things felt uncertain. The future looked shaky. And God, through Isaiah, said, "I'm going to give you a sign." That sign? A child—born to a young woman—will be named Immanuel. That name, Immanuel, is powerful. It means God with us. It's more than a label—it's a reminder. God isn't distant or passive. God is right in the middle of your real life, your stress, your joy, your mess. Immanuel isn't just what Jesus

REFLECT

was called—it's who God is. Then and now. This prophecy was for that king, but more importantly, it pointed ahead to something much bigger. Hundreds of years later, Jesus was born. The promise came true. Even when people were scared, confused, or unsure, God was already working. Advent reminds us that even in the waiting, God is faithful. Even in the unknown, God is already with us. Already planning. Already present. If "God with us" is true, how would that shift the way you see your current circumstances?

I can't tell the future, but I bet the question you get asked most during the month of December is, "What do you want for Christmas?" While you may have a list ready for when people ask you, have you ever thought about how WITH could be the best gift you could ever give? Being with people can be the best gift you ever give! Don't overthink the idea of WITH. How can you share some of your time with the people in your life who might need it most? What will you move off your calendar so that you can spend an hour with someone?

Day 1

READ

Hope Has a Name

The people walking in darkness have seen a great light. On those living in a pitch-dark land, light has dawned. A child is born to us, a son is given to us, and authority will be on his shoulders. He will be named Wonderful Counselor, Mighty God, Eternal Father, Prince of Peace. There will be vast authority and endless peace for David's throne and for his kingdom, establishing and sustaining it with justice and righteousness now and forever. ISAIAH 9:2, 6-7 CEB

REFLECT

Isaiah wrote these words hundreds of years before Jesus was born. The world was a mess! People were hurting, wondering if things would ever get better. Sound familiar? But then, hope. Not a concept, not a motivational quote, but a person. The prophet Isaiah says a child will be born, and this child will carry names that change everything:

Wonderful Counselor, God listens to you

Mighty God: God is strong enough to carry what you can't.
Eternal Father: God never gives up on you.
Prince of Peace: God can bring calm to your chaos.

Jesus is the light Isaiah was talking about. He's not just a past promise—He's a present hope. Which name for Jesus stands out to you the most right now, and why do you need that version of Him in your life?

Art can become light when you use it to lift someone else up! Choose one name of Jesus from Isaiah 9: Wonderful Counselor, Mighty God, Eternal Father, or Prince of Peace. Write it out on a small piece of paper or index card, and add simple artwork around it with colors, symbols, or designs that reflect what it means. Give your art to someone who needs encouragement this week. Slide it into a locker, hand it to a friend, or leave it where someone will find it. You're planting hope in someone's life by reminding them who Jesus is.

Day 2

Micah's words weren't spoken in a peaceful time. His people were experiencing fear, war, and uncertainty. Things were falling apart. But even in the middle of all that chaos, Micah speaks hope: A ruler will come from Bethlehem. A shepherd. A source of peace. That's bold. And beautiful. Micah gave this prophecy long before Jesus was born, pointing to a tiny, overlooked town called Bethlehem. Not exactly the place people expected a King to show up. It was small. Quiet. Easy to miss. But God chose Bethlehem on purpose. That's how God works. God often chooses the

Small Place—Big Promise

As for you, Bethlehem of Ephrathah, though you are the least significant of Judah's forces, one who is to be a ruler in Israel on my behalf will come out from you. His origin is from remote times, from ancient days. Therefore, he will give them up until the time when she who is in labor gives birth The rest of his kin will return to the people of Israel. MICAH 5:2-3 CEB unexpected—the people and places others overlook—to do something huge. Bethlehem wasn't famous or fancy, but it became the birthplace of hope. A reminder that small doesn't mean insignificant. During this Advent season, we see lots of reminders that God can use any place, any person, or any moment to do incredible things in the world. Where in your life do you feel small or unnoticed? What might it mean to believe God can still work through you?

RESPOND

Sometimes the best way to give someone hope is by believing in them and giving them something significant to participate in. In fact, at times, asking for help can give someone more hope than actually helping them. Today, ask someone for help. It can be as simple as asking someone to help with your homework or as big as being honest with someone about something you are struggling with. You may be surprised how it brightens their day.

Day 3

God Shows Up in the Ordinary

When Elizabeth was six months pregnant, God sent the angel Gabriel to Nazareth, a city in Galilee, to a virgin who was engaged to a man named Joseph, a descendant of David's house. The virgin's name was Mary. When the angel came to her, he said, "Rejoice, favored one! The Lord is with you!" She was confused by these words and wondered what kind of greeting this might be. The angel said, "Don't be afraid, Mary. God is honoring you. Look! You will conceive and give birth to a son, and you will name him Jesus. He will be great and he will be called the Son of the Most High. The Lord God will give him the throne of David his father. He will rule over Jacob's house forever, and there will be no end to his kingdom. LUKE 1:26-33 CEB

READ

Mary was just a regular girl in a small, quiet town. She wasn't rich, famous, or powerful. She was engaged and probably dreaming about her future with Joseph when everything changed. God

REFLE

...CT

sent an angel with a message that would completely flip her life upside down. This moment reminds us that God often shows up in the ordinary, in the middle of normal days, and calls regular people into extraordinary things. Mary didn't feel ready. She was confused and afraid. But the angel said, "Rejoice! The Lord is with you." Here's the truth: you don't have to be perfect or have it all together for God to show up in your life. God sees you, honors you, and invites you to be part of something bigger than yourself. Where in your ordinary life might God be showing up right now?

RESPOND

Today, you get to show up in the middle of someone's ordinary life. Think of a friend or a family member who needs to be reminded that they are loved. Get specific. Why is this person special to you? Then send that video! I promise you that you just made someone's day!

Day 4

Questions, Faith, and a Brave, Yes!

Then Mary said to the angel, "How will this happen since I haven't had sexual relations with a man?" The angel replied, "The Holy Spirit will come over you and the power of the Most High will overshadow you. Therefore, the one who is to be born will be holy. He will be called God's Son. Look, even in her old age, your relative Elizabeth has conceived a son. This woman, who was labeled 'unable to conceive,' is now six months pregnant. Nothing is impossible for God." Then Mary said, "I am the Lord's servant. Let it be with me just as you have said." Then the angel left her. LUKE 1:34-38 CEB

Mary didn't fake it. She didn't pretend to understand or immediately say, "Sounds great!" She asked a real question: "How is this even going to happen?" And honestly? Fair. What the angel told her didn't make sense. It felt impossible. But here's the beautiful part: God didn't shut her down. The angel gave her a glimpse of the bigger picture. A reminder that God was already doing something miraculous through Elizabeth, and that nothing is impossible for God. Mary didn't get every answer, but she trusted God enough to say yes anyway. "Let it

READ

REFLECT

be with me just as you have said. That's courage. That's faith. Advent reminds us that asking questions doesn't mean we lack faith. It's part of the journey. And sometimes, faith looks like saying yes before we know how it all turns out. *What's something in your life that feels impossible right now, and what might it look like to trust God with it?*

RESPOND

Let's get into the Christmas spirit! Plan a movie night to watch your favorite Christmas movie. Who needs to get in the Christmas spirit? Do you have an older neighbor who would love to experience the joy of hanging around with your family? Do you have a friend who needs some extra cheer? Pick a movie. Plan the snacks and get to inviting!

Day 5

Right after hearing life-changing news, Mary didn't sit still; she hurried to see Elizabeth. Why? Maybe she needed someone who would understand. Someone who wouldn't think she was crazy. Someone who was also living a miracle. And Elizabeth got it. The moment Mary walked in, Elizabeth celebrated her. No judgment. No doubt. Just joy and encouragement. We all need people like that friend who celebrates what God is doing in us, who cheers us on when we take a step of faith, and who speaks truth over us when we feel overwhelmed. Who in your

When You Need Someone Who Gets It

Mary got up and hurried to a city in the Judean highlands. She entered Zechariah's home and greeted Elizabeth. When Elizabeth heard Mary's greeting, the child leaped in her womb, and Elizabeth was filled with the Holy Spirit. With a loud voice she blurted out, "God has blessed you above all women, and he has blessed the child you carry. Why do I have this honor, that the mother of my Lord should come to me? As soon as I heard your greeting, the baby in my womb jumped for joy. Hap██ is

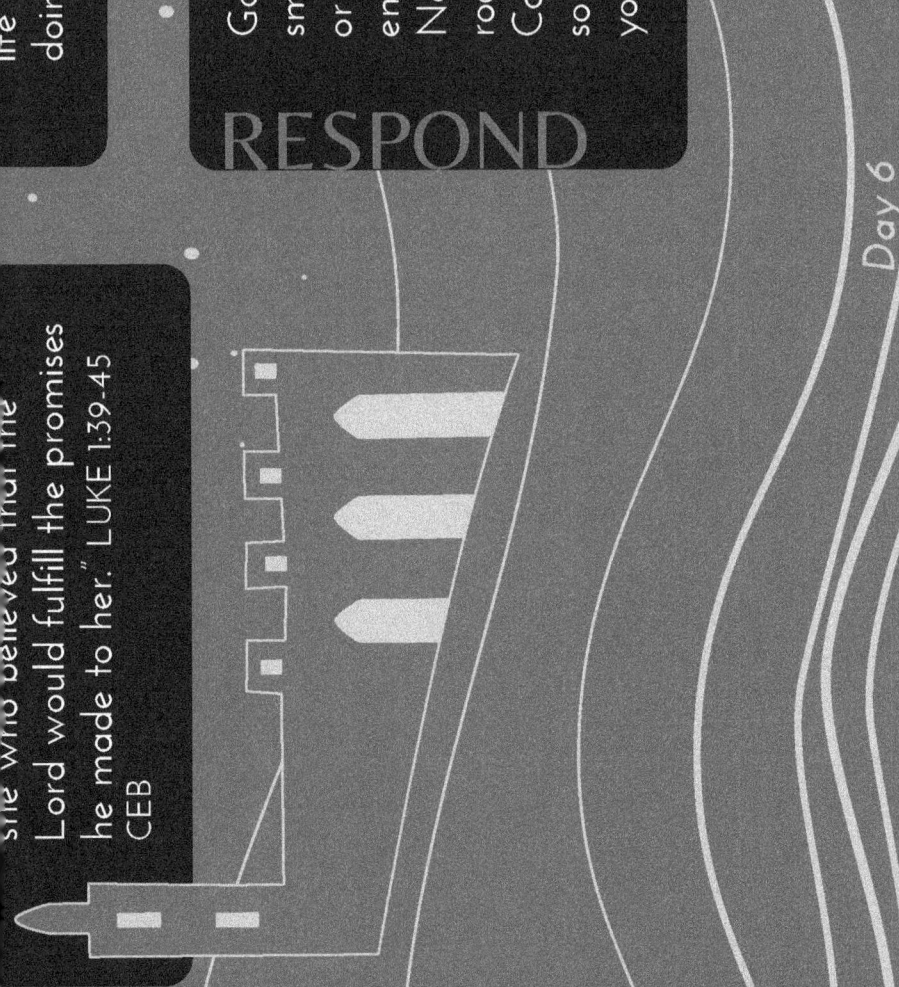

life helps you see what God is doing in you?

RESPOND

Go out and find some larger smooth rocks. Using a marker or paint, write messages of encouragement on the rocks. Now go to a park with your rocks and spread them around. Can you imagine how happy someone will be when they see your kind words?

she who believed that the Lord would fulfill the promises he made to her." LUKE 1:39-45 CEB

Day 6

More Surprises

Mary stayed with Elizabeth about three months, and then returned to her home. When the time came for Elizabeth to have her child, she gave birth to a boy. Her neighbors and relatives celebrated with her because they had heard that the Lord had shown her great mercy. On the eighth day, it came time to circumcise the child. They wanted to name him Zechariah because that was his father's name. But his mother replied, "No, his name will be John." They said to her, "None of your relatives have that name." Then they began gesturing to his father to see what he wanted to call him. After asking for a tablet, he surprised everyone by writing, "His name is John." LUKE 1:56-63 CEB

Mary stayed with Elizabeth for three months, most likely right up until her baby was born. She witnessed firsthand what it looks like when God's promises come true! When the baby arrived, the people around Elizabeth expected things to go the usual way, naming the baby after his dad. But Elizabeth, and then Zechariah said something different. "His name is John." It surprised everyone

CT

Sometimes trusting God means taking a path others don't expect. It might not make sense to the people around you, but obedience isn't about fitting in; it's about being faithful to what God has spoken. Often, that takes courage. Have you ever felt like doing the right thing made you stand out? How did you handle it?

RESPOND

Being around our friends is a comfortable experience. That's why we stay with the people who know us. But today you are going to step out of your comfortable circle. Sit next to someone whom you noticed is alone. Say hi to someone you don't know very well. Text or DM someone to hang out with who could become a new friend. You may be surprised by how stepping out of your comfort zone could lead to meaningful connections.

READ

This Was NOT the Plan

In those days, Caesar Augustus declared that everyone throughout the empire should be enrolled in the tax lists. This first enrollment occurred when Quirinius governed Syria. Everyone went to their own cities to be enrolled. Since Joseph belonged to David's house and family line, he went up from the city of Nazareth in Galilee to David's city, called Bethlehem, in Judea. He went to be enrolled together with Mary, who was promised to him in marriage and who was pregnant.
LUKE 2:1-5 CEB

REFLECT

So here's what went down: the emperor decided everyone had to go back to their hometown to be counted (like an ancient version of the census). That meant Joseph had to travel to Bethlehem, and Mary, very pregnant, had to go with him. This was not a quick road trip. It's about 90 miles. On foot. While pregnant. Not exactly ideal for an impromptu road trip. Mary and Joseph probably thought they'd have their baby at home, surrounded by family and comfort. But instead they were on the road, in a crowd, heading toward the unknown. It had to feel confusing, uncomfortable, and definitely not how they imagined things going. And yet...this was exactly where God needed them to be. Advent reminds us that even when life feels chaotic or out of place, God is still working behind the scenes. Has anything in your life ever gone totally off script but worked out in a surprising way?

RESPOND

Grab a couple of trash bags and hit the streets! Anytime we are in creation, it points back to our Creator, God. Keeping creation clean is important; I don't have to tell you that, though! You can start with the street in front of your house, and when you are ready, head to the local park. Fill up the trash bags and keep your community clean!

REFLECT

We both know you have clothes that you don't wear. Find five things you don't wear that are clean and still look nice. Put them in a bag and donate them to a local shelter. If you have more than five pieces, go big and stuff an entire garbage bag full!

READ

God Joins the Chat

While they were there, the time came for Mary to have her baby. She gave birth to her firstborn child, a son, wrapped him snugly, and laid him in a manger, because there was no place for them in the guestroom. LUKE 2:6-7 CEB

RESPON

Mary and Joseph finally made it to Bethlehem...and there was no place for them to stay. No guest room. No comfy bed. Just a spot where animals lived. That's where Mary gave birth to Jesus.

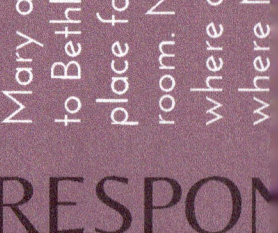

Let that sink in: The Son of God was born in a place that probably smelled like hay, sweat, and animals. It was messy, uncomfortable, and far from perfect. But that's exactly where God chose to enter the world. God didn't wait for perfect conditions. God showed up right in the middle of the chaos. And the same is true today—God doesn't need your life to be tidy, polished, or put together. God is for you. Period. Where in your life does it feel a little messy right now? What would it mean to share that with God?

READ

Good News for the Underdog

Nearby, shepherds were living in the fields, guarding their sheep at night. The Lord's angel stood before them, the Lord's glory shone around them, and they were terrified. The angel said, "Don't be afraid! Look! I bring good news to you—wonderful, joyous news for all people. Your savior is born today in David's city. He is Christ the Lord. This is a sign for you: you will find a newborn baby wrapped snugly and lying in a manger." LUKE 2:8-12 CEB

REFLECT

Out in the fields, a group of shepherds were just doing their job watching sheep, probably half-asleep, when boom, an angel shows up and lights up the night. The angel said, "Don't freak out! I've got good news that will bring great joy to all people." And here's the twist: the first people to hear about Jesus being born weren't kings or religious leaders. They were shepherds—

RESPOND

Wherever you go to school, there is a human who cleans it. If you do not know who cleans up this space, now is the time to find out! You get to celebrate these humans by reminding them that the work they do is appreciated. You can write them a letter and stuff an envelope with confetti. You could bake them cookies. You could pick up a box of your favorite Christmas candy. You pick! It is the act of celebrating these wonderful people that matters most.

regular, overlooked, probably—not-invited-to-most-parties kind of people. God could have announced Jesus' birth to anyone, but God chose the Shepherd very intentionally. When we read this story about the Shepherds, it is a great time to remember that the Bible was written to free oppressed people. From the beginning of Jesus' life, he showed up for the least likely humans. This move was God reminding us that Jesus is FOR EVERYONE. Full stop. What would change if you really believed God notices you, even when no one else does?

Day 10

Sometimes You Have to See It For Yourself

When the angels returned to heaven, the shepherds said to each other, "Let's go right now to Bethlehem and see what's happened. Let's confirm what the Lord has revealed to us." They went quickly and found Mary and Joseph, and the baby lying in the manger. When they saw this, they reported what they had been told about this child. Everyone who heard it was amazed at what the shepherds told them. Mary committed these things to memory and considered them carefully. The shepherds returned home, glorifying and praising God for all they had heard and seen. Everything happened just as they had been told. LUKE 2:15-20 CEB

After the angels left, they didn't say, "Cool story," and get back to sheep duty. They hurried to find Mary, Joseph, and baby Jesus because they had to see it for themselves. And when they found Jesus, they couldn't keep it to themselves. They told everyone what they'd seen and heard. Meanwhile, the shepherds went back to their lives, still praising God, changed by what they had experienced. Sometimes it's not enough to hear about God; you've got to go see for yourself.

even closer than you thought. Faith isn't something we just hear about; it is something that we get to experience. What's one way you can lean in and "go see for yourself" who Jesus is this Advent season?

RESPOND

Today, look for signs of God's presence in your own home. You don't have to go anywhere to "see for yourself"; God shows up in everyday spaces when we're paying attention. Choose a moment today, maybe in the morning, at mealtime, or before bed. No matter what time you choose to do this, you need to pause to slow down and notice what's around you. Look for the good around you, like when someone in your family uses encouraging words or does a random act of kindness. Look for something that reminds you of God's care. Then I want you to capture it! Write it down, take a picture, or draw it. Once you have captured the moment, share it with your people with this sentence: "Here is where I saw God today." The shepherds found Jesus in an ordinary place, a stable. You can find God in the ordinary moments of your life, too! Sometimes all it takes is slowing down to notice it!

Eight days after Jesus was born, Mary and Joseph followed through with something simple but important: they had Him circumcised and named Him Jesus, just like the angel told them. Then they went to the temple to offer a sacrifice, as the law said they should. It might seem like a small moment in the bigger story, but it shows us something powerful. Mary and Joseph were faithful in the little things. No spotlight. No angels this time. Just mundane obedience. Sometimes following God doesn't look flashy. Instead, it's simply showing up, doing the next, right thing. Faith isn't always dramatic; it shows up in the small

Ordinary Faith

When eight days had passed, Jesus' parents circumcised him and gave him the name Jesus. This was the name given to him by the angel before he was conceived. When the time came for their ritual cleansing, in accordance with the Law from Moses, they brought Jesus up to Jerusalem to present him to the Lord. (It's written in the Law of the Lord, "Every firstborn male will be dedicated to the Lord.") They offered a sacrifice in keeping with what's stated in the Law of the Lord, A pair of turtledoves or two young pigeons.
LUKE 2:21-24 CEB

choices we make every day. What's something quiet but meaningful you could do today to stay close to Jesus?

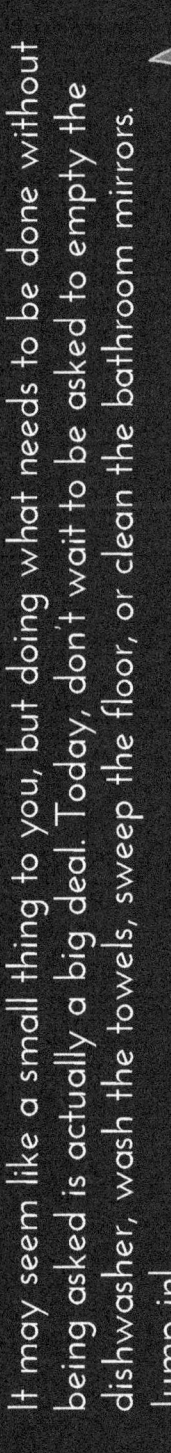

It may seem like a small thing to you, but doing what needs to be done without being asked is actually a big deal. Today, don't wait to be asked to empty the dishwasher, wash the towels, sweep the floor, or clean the bathroom mirrors. Jump in!

RESPOND

Day 12

READ

The Search

After Jesus was born in Bethlehem in the territory of Judea during the rule of King Herod, magi came from the east to Jerusalem. MATTHEW 2:1 CEB

REFLECT

Jesus had just been born, and far away somewhere in the east, a group of magi (think wise scholars) noticed something different in the sky. They packed up and traveled a long way to find "The One" who had been born King of the Jews. They didn't know exactly where they were going. They didn't have all the answers. But they were willing to search. That's what faith looks like sometimes. You don't have it all figured out, but you're still hungry for something real, something more. You crave something authentic. That is often when the journey to Jesus begins. It doesn't matter if your search is full of detours and uncertainty. What matters is that you keep searching. Where in your life do you feel like you're searching? How is God inviting you to keep going?

Christmas showcases people's personal decor choices, especially when it comes to how people decorate their homes and yards. Does a yard full of themed blow-ups bring you joy? Is it a home decorated in soft white lights, bringing you all the cozy vibes? Lights and music timed to your favorite songs might be catching your attention this year. Whatever it is, pick your favorite. Make some sort of trophy and take it to your favorite house with an adult! I know you will bring so much happiness to the person who took a lot of pride in decorating their home.

RESPOND

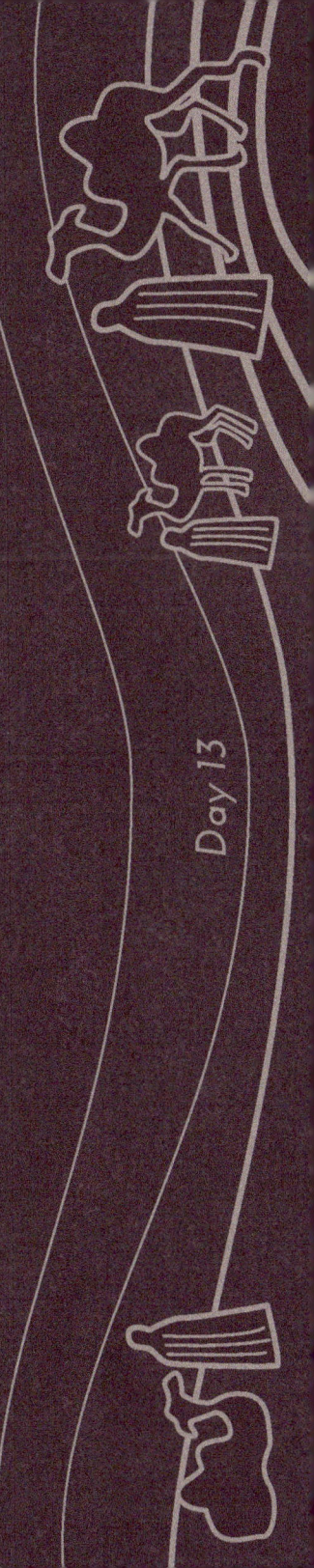

Day 13

Not Everyone is Excited

When King Herod heard this, he was troubled, and everyone in Jerusalem was troubled with him. He gathered all the chief priests and the legal experts and asked them where the Christ was to be born. They said, "In Bethlehem of Judea, for this is what the prophet wrote: You, Bethlehem, land of Judah, by no means are you the least among the rulers of Judah, because from you will come one who governs, who will shepherd my people Israel."

Then Herod secretly called for the magi and found out from them the time when the star had first appeared. He sent them to Bethlehem, saying, "Go and search carefully for the child. When you've found him, report to me so that I too may go and honor him." MATTHEW 2:3-8 CEB

When King Herod heard about the birth of Jesus, he wasn't excited—he was troubled. And not just him, everyone around him started freaking out too. Herod wasn't looking for hope. He was trying to hold onto power. King Herod devised a sneaky plan: tell the magi to find the baby,

REFL

men report back so he could honor him. Spoiler: he wasn't going to honor baby Jesus. This part of the story is a reminder that not everyone celebrates what God is doing. Sometimes, people are more interested in control than in change. This move by King Herod reminds us that real hope can be disruptive, but it is worth searching for! Have you ever felt unsure about following Jesus because of how others might react? What helps you stay focused anyway?

RESPOND

Sometimes, bringing hope takes courage. Sticky notes are going to be the tool that brings some beautiful truths to the humans in your life. Write words of encouragement on a couple of sticky notes and leave them for your friends! What if you put some sticky notes on the mirror in the bathroom at your school to remind your friends that they are incredible humans!

Day 14

REFLECT

After their conversation with Herod, the magi kept moving. And then, it happened! That same star they saw in the east showed up again, leading the way straight to Jesus. When they saw the star, they were filled with joy. They didn't have GPS. They didn't know the full plan. But they had a light, and they followed it. And when it finally brought them close to Jesus, their response wasn't just relief. It was pure joy. Sometimes, life feels like wandering. You're not sure what's next or where you're headed. You don't have a set of directions to lead every step, and that can be frustrating. When we

READ

Magi on the Move

When they heard the king, they went; and look, the star they had seen in the east went ahead of them until it stood over the place where the child was. When they saw the star, they were filled with joy. MATTHEW 2:9-10 CEB

RESPON

When families are in crisis, children can often be moved from their homes to a safe place. When this happens, they are moved without their personal things. Today, you are going to donate pajamas to foster care don't know the next, connecting with God can be how you find direction. Keep facing the light and allow it to lead you. This can look like continuing to be kind even when it feels like life is being unkind to you. What's the "light" in your life right now, something that's helping you stay close to Jesus?

You may have some in your room that you have never used, or you may need to ask an adult to take you to the store to buy some. There will be a local foster care location where you can take your pajamas.

Day 15

READ

Worship Shows Up

They entered the house and saw the child with Mary, his mother. Falling to their knees, they honored him. Then they opened their treasure chests and presented him with gifts of gold, frankincense, and myrrh. Because they were warned in a dream not to return to Herod, they went back to their own country by another route. MATTHEW 2:11-12 CEB

REFLECT

When the magi finally arrived, they saw Jesus, and immediately bowed down and worshipped Him. But they didn't stop there. They opened their treasure chests and gave Him gifts: gold, frankincense, and myrrh—expensive and thoughtful gifts for a King. Then, when it was time to leave, they didn't go back the way they came. God warned them in a dream

RESPOND

An entire meal. Yep, you are going to cook an entire meal for your family. If your family is on the go this week, then cook a meal to give to a friend. Do your best, and know whoever gets the chance to eat this meal will love it!

and they listened. They took a different road to avoid any conflict with King Herod. Their whole journey, searching, giving, obeying, was an act of worship. Worship isn't just about singing songs. It's about offering your best, your attention, your heart. It's about letting an encounter with Jesus change your direction. What's something valuable (your time, attention, creativity, etc.) you could offer to Jesus this week?

Day 16

READ

Plans Change

When the magi had departed, an angel from the Lord appeared to Joseph in a dream and said, "Get up. Take the child and his mother and escape to Egypt. Stay there until I tell you, for Herod will soon search for the child in order to kill him." Joseph got up and, during the night, took the child and his mother to Egypt. He stayed there until Herod died. This fulfilled what the Lord had spoken through the prophet: I have called my son out of Egypt. MATTHEW 2:13-15 CEB

REFLECT

Just when things seemed to settle down, everything changed again. An angel appeared to Joseph in a dream and said, "Get up. Take the child and His mother and escape to Egypt." King Herod was insecure and was planning to hurt Jesus. The only way to stay safe was to leave immediately! So Joseph didn't wait. He got up that night and left for Egypt. Sometimes following God means being flexible, especially when plans change fast. It's not always comfortable. It doesn't always make sense. But when Joseph heard God say, "Move," he decided that protecting his family was more important than his personal comfort. When life takes a turn you didn't see coming, what helps you remember that God is still with you?

Today, we get to see what kind of wrapping skills you have! You are going to offer to wrap all the gifts you can in your house. Are you feeling like a master wrapper? Ask your grandparents or a family friend if you can come spend the day wrapping gifts for them, too!

RESPOND

Day 17

After Herod died, an angel told Joseph it was safe to go back home. But when he heard Herod's son was ruling, Joseph got nervous. So God warned him again in a dream, so they changed their destination again. They decided the safest place to move would be to Nazareth. Joseph probably thought he'd go back to where it all started, but God led them somewhere new. It was still home, just not the one they expected. Sometimes, we end up in places we didn't plan. Life shifts, doors close, and we find ourselves in Nazareth instead of Bethlehem. Nazareth became the hometown of Jesus. The new plan was always

A Home

After King Herod died, an angel from the Lord appeared in a dream to Joseph in Egypt. "Get up," the angel said, "and take the child and his mother and go to the land of Israel. Those who were trying to kill the child are dead." Joseph got up, took the child and his mother, and went to the land of Israel. But when he heard that Archelaus ruled over Judea in place of his father Herod, Joseph was afraid to go there. Having been warned in a dream, he went to the area of Galilee. He settled in a city called Nazareth so that what was spoken through

...part of God's plan. Even when our journey changes, God is still guiding our story. Have you ever ended up somewhere different from what you planned, emotionally, spiritually, or even physically? What might God be doing in this "new place"?

...the prophets might be fulfilled: He will be called a Nazarene.
MATTHEW 2:19-23 CEB

RESPOND

Food banks serve as a place of refuge when families need support. Most communities have a food bank that is accessible to all humans. Collect some canned food, pet food, diapers, or toothpaste that you can donate to a place in your community. Want to go to the next level? Organize your friends and family to reach a goal of 100 items collected!

Day 18

Make Room

READ

John went throughout the region of the Jordan River, calling for people to be baptized to show that they were changing their hearts and lives and wanted God to forgive their sins. This is just as it was written in the scroll of the words of Isaiah the prophet, A voice crying out in the wilderness: "Prepare the way for the Lord; make his paths straight. Every valley will be filled, and every mountain and hill will be leveled. The crooked will be made straight and the rough places made smooth. All humanity will see God's salvation." LUKE 3:2-6 CEB

REFLECT

Remember back on Day 3 when Mary visited her cousin Elizabeth, and the baby leapt in Elizabeth's womb? That baby was John the Baptist. Now, he's all grown up, living in the wilderness, and doing exactly what he was born to do: help people get ready for Jesus. John wasn't trying to be famous. He was focused. His message was clear: "Prepare the way for the Lord; make his paths straight." His whole job was to help people make room, clear out the distractions, and open their hearts to the One who was coming. That call still matters today. Advent isn't just about remembering Jesus was born; it's about getting ready for Him to show up in our everyday lives. Advent reminds us that preparation isn't about perfection, it's about making space. What's something in your life that might be getting in the way of really seeing or hearing Jesus?

RESPOND

Just as John helped people make space for Jesus, today you will find a way to make room for someone else. You can help "make room" for someone by stepping into their stress and sharing the load, especially when they're overwhelmed. Think of someone in your life who seems stretched thin or stressed out, like a friend drowning in homework or a caregiver juggling too much. Don't just say, "Let me know if you need anything." That puts the pressure on them. Instead, say something like, "Can I quiz you for your test tomorrow?" or "I've got time after school, can I help you clean up your room/office?" Don't forget to follow through. You showing up and offering help might be the best gift this season!

READ

All In

At that time, Jesus came from Galilee to the Jordan River so that John would baptize him. John tried to stop him and said, "I need to be baptized by you, yet you come to me?" Jesus answered, "Allow me to be baptized now. This is necessary to fulfill all righteousness." So John agreed to baptize Jesus. When Jesus was baptized, he immediately came up out of the water. Heaven was opened to him, and he saw the Spirit of God coming down like a dove and resting on him. A voice from heaven said, "This is my Son whom I dearly love; I find happiness in him." MATTHEW 3:13-17 CEB

REFLECT

Yesterday, we talked about how John the Baptist, Jesus' cousin, spent his life preparing people to meet the Messiah. He called people to change their ways and turn towards God. Often, people marked this change by being baptized. Then one day, something surprising happened. Jesus showed up and asked John to baptize Him. John was like, "Wait, me baptize you?" But Jesus said, "This is the right way." So John did! He baptized Jesus in the river, and something incredible happened. As Jesus came up from the water, the heavens opened. The Spirit of God came down like a dove. And a voice said, "This is my Son, whom I dearly love. I find happiness in Him." This moment marked the beginning of Jesus' public ministry. Jesus' ministry in the world began with obedience, humility, and a clear declaration of identity. What's something you're afraid to start, but deep down, you know God's calling you to it?

RESPOND

Jesus didn't just talk about showing up—He stepped into the water and went all in. Today is the day you get to go all in on the refrigerator! Take everything out. Clean the inside out, then wipe everything off before putting it away. If you think something looks like your science experiment from second grade, ask an adult if it is ok if you toss it out.

READ

More Than a Manger

The Son is the image of the invisible God, the one who is first over all creation, because all things were created by him: both in the heavens and on the earth the things that are visible and the things that are invisible. Whether they are thrones or powers, or rulers or authorities, all things were created through him and for him. He existed before all things, and all things are held together in him. He is the head of the body, the church, who is the beginning, the one who is firstborn from among the dead so that he might occupy the first place in everything.
COLOSSIANS 1:15-18 CEB

REFLECT

When you think of Jesus during Advent, it's easy to picture a baby in a manger, wrapped in cloth, surrounded by animals and sleepy shepherds. But this passage? It zooms way out and shows us a much bigger view of who Jesus is. He's the image of the invisible God. He created everything—everything you can see and everything you can't. He existed before anything else. And He's the one holding everything together. Read that again: holding everything together. That means your future? Your questions? Your stress? He's holding that, too. Jesus isn't just a historical figure or someone we sing about at Christmas. He's the center of everything—past, present, and future. Jesus chose to come close. He chose to be born into our world, not because He had to, but because He loves you. Write down something in your life that feels out of control right now. How does it change things to know Jesus is holding it all together?

RESPOND

Sometimes the best way to help someone feel held is by sharing peace—not fixing, just reminding. This week, try a breath prayer and pass it on:

- [INHALE] Jesus, You hold all things together.
- [EXHALE] Hold me, and help me hold space for others.
- Repeat slowly until your body and heart rest in the truth.

Then share it with someone who may be stressed, overwhelmed, or quiet. Write it on a sticky note, card, or paper and leave it for them. If they're far away, send a text like: "I prayed this today. Maybe it'll help you breathe, too." You don't need all the answers to bring peace. Sometimes the simplest words—the ones we breathe—remind someone they're not alone.

READ

God is Full Color

In the past, God spoke through the prophets to our ancestors in many times and many ways. In these final days, though, he spoke to us through a Son. God made his Son the heir of everything and created the world through him. The Son is the light of God's glory and the imprint of God's being. He maintains everything with his powerful message. After he carried out the cleansing of people from their sins, he sat down at the right side of the highest majesty. And the Son became so much greater than the other messengers, such as angels, that he received a more important title than theirs. HEBREWS 1:1-4 CEB

RESPOND

When you give something away with purpose and love, you're reminding someone: God sees you, and so do I. Head into your room and search for four items you no longer need, items that no longer serve you. These could be gently

REFLECT

God has always been speaking, through creation, through the prophets, through moments in history. But in these verses, the writer of Hebrews tells us something incredible: Now, God speaks through the Son. Jesus is loved toys that you could clean up and donate to a local shelter. Do you have lotion and soap that you never used? The local food bank takes personal hygiene products to give to its clients. What you give away doesn't have to be big or fancy; it just needs to be thoughtful and intentional.

God's voice. God's message. God's heart in full color. Jesus is the radiance of God's glory. The exact imprint of who God is. That means if you've ever wondered what God is like, you don't have to guess. Look at Jesus. He didn't just come to represent God; Jesus came to reveal Him completely. If Jesus shows us exactly what God is like... what does that change about how you see God?

Day 22

Our Neighborhood

READ

The Word became flesh and made his home among us. We have seen his glory, glory like that of a father's only son, full of grace and truth. JOHN 1:14 CEB

The Word became flesh and blood, and moved into the neighborhood. We saw the glory with our own eyes, the one-of-a-kind glory, like Father, like Son, Generous inside and out, true from start to finish. JOHN 1:14 MSG

REFLECT

Out of all the ways John could describe Jesus' birth, he chose this: God moved in-into our world, our space, our mess, and our everyday lives. Jesus didn't show up in a castle or on a stage. He came as a baby, born in a borrowed room, wrapped in love. He set up camp right where we live. The Message translation says, "He moved into the neighborhood." That means Jesus didn't come to stay distant or unreachable. He came to be close—to walk the same roads, face the same struggles, feel the same feelings. He became our neighbor. What would change if you lived like Jesus was actually your neighbor?

RESPOND

Jesus didn't just talk about love. He moved in and showed up for people in real, everyday ways. When you show kindness to the people around you, you reflect the heart of Jesus. This week, take that love into your neighborhood. Grab a broom or a shovel (depending on the weather!) and go make a difference right outside your door. Choose one simple way to serve: sweep a neighbor's porch or walkway, shovel snow from a sidewalk or driveway, pick up trash around your block or in a nearby park, or rake leaves from a yard that's been ignored. You don't have to announce it. Do it with love, and let your actions speak!

Day 23

REFLECT

As we close out Advent, this Psalm gives us one final, beautiful truth: Jesus didn't just come to save us; He came to make things right. Psalm 96 paints a picture of the whole world celebrating, not just because a King is born, but because that King will bring justice to everyone. That means wrong things will be made right. Broken systems will be healed. People who've been overlooked, silenced, or hurt will be seen and restored. This joy doesn't come from avoiding pain; it's the result of confronting pain with healing and hope. Advent reminds us that the joy Jesus brings isn't exclusive; it's for all people.

READ

Joy and Justice

Tell the nations, "The Lord rules! Yes, he set the world firmly in place; it won't be shaken. He will judge all people fairly." Let heaven celebrate! Let the earth rejoice! Let the sea and everything in it roar! Let the countryside and everything in it celebrate! Then all the trees of the forest too will shout out joyfully before the Lord because he is coming! He is coming to establish justice on the earth! He will establish justice in the world rightly. He will establish justice among all people fairly. PSALMS 96:10-13 CE

When that joy is rooted in justice, it's the kind of joy that is stable enough to endure the hard times. What's one thing in your community that you long for Jesus to make right? How can you be part of that work?

Day 24

RESPOND

Take the time to light your candle today with your family or friends. As your candle burns, read aloud the Christmas story. Try reading from both Luke 2:1-20 CEB and Matthew 1:18-2:23 The Message. Take time to reflect on what you have learned through the last 23 days as you grew through your Advent journey.

A Christmas Blessing

May you feel the nearness of Jesus today. Not just in the music or lights, but in the places that ache for healing and hope. May His joy meet you in the struggle. May His peace stretch beyond comfort to courage. May His justice stir something bold in you. A vision for a world where every voice is heard, every person is seen. And as you celebrate today, may you remember that Jesus didn't just come to make life sweeter, He came to make it just and right. May you carry His light into dark places. May you speak up, lift up, and show up with love that looks like action and hope that moves with purpose.

Merry Christmas. The Light has come. Jesus is calling you to reflect that Light.

Day 25

RESPOND

RESPOND

RESPOND

www.ingramcontent.com/pod-product-compliance
Lightning Source LLC
Chambersburg PA
CBHW051340120626
46547CB00016B/2618